SACRAMENTO PUBLIC LIBRARY

3 3029 06136 1168

SACRAMENTO PUBLIC LIBRARY
828 "I" STREET
SACRAMENTO, CA 95814

7/2008

D0468524

THE SEASHORE

A Saltwater Web of Life

Philip Johansson

Enslow Elementary

an imprint of

Enslow Publishers, Inc.

40 Industrial Road
Box 398
Berkeley Heights, NJ 07922
USA

http://www.enslow.com

Copyright © 2008 by Philip Johansson

All rights reserved.

No part of this book may be reproduced by any means without the written permission of the publisher.

Library of Congress Cataloging-in-Publication Data

Johansson, Philip.
   The seashore: a saltwater web of life / Philip Johansson.
      p. cm. — (Wonderful water biomes)
      Summary: "Provides information about the biome of the seashore following the
food web and flow of energy from sun to plants and animals"—Provided by publisher.
   Includes bibliographical references and index.
   ISBN-13: 978-0-7660-2811-1
   ISBN-10: 0-7660-2811-9
   1. Seashore ecology—Juvenile literature. I. Title.
   QH541.5.S35J64 2008
   577.69'9—dc22

                                                        2006100600

Printed in the United States of America

10 9 8 7 6 5 4 3 2 1

To Our Readers: We have done our best to make sure all Internet Addresses in this book were active and appropriate when we went to press. However, the author and the publisher have no control over and assume no liability for the material available on those Internet sites or on other Web sites they may link to. Any comments or suggestions can be sent by e-mail to comments@enslow.com or to the address on the back cover.

Every effort has been made to locate all copyright holders of material used in this book. If any errors or omissions have occurred, corrections will be made in future editions of this book.

Illustration Credits: Copyright © 1987, 1998 by Dover Publications, Inc.

Photo Credits: Adam Jones/Photo Researchers, Inc., p. 31; Animals Animals: © Anne W. Rosenfeld, p. 40, © Doug Wechsler, p. 44 (gull), © James Watt, p. 30, © Mike Norton, p. 32, © Patti Murray, pp. 20, 44 (beach grass), © Randy Morse, pp. 21, 25 (middle), 44 (sea urchin); Bill Frank, Jacksonville, Florida, p. 44 (mole crab); Frank Paladino, pp. 4, 7; © 2006/Frans Lanting, pp. 8, 9, 35; Gary Shrimpling, pp. 15, 25 (top); Jim D. Barr/Alaskastock.com, p. 13; © 2006 Jupiterimages Corporation, pp. 12, 18; © Neil Bromhall/Naturepl.com, p. 41; Shutterstock, pp. 22, 25 (bottom), 43; Tom McHugh/Photo Researchers, Inc., p. 42; Visuals Unlimited: © Brandon Cole, p. 29, © David Wrobel, p. 17, © Diane Nelson, p. 44 (water bear), © Dr. John D. Cunningham, p. 44 (sand flea), © Richard Hermann, pp. 28, 33, © Rick Poley, 36, © Robert DeGoursey, p. 38, © Dr. Stanley Flegler, p. 27; Wikipedia, p. 24.

Front Cover: (*clockwise from upper left*) John Cornell/Visuals Unlimited; Shutterstock; Animals Animals, © Doug Wechsler; Shutterstock.

Back Cover: © 2006 Jupiterimages Corporation.

Dr. Frank Paladino is a herpetologist at Indiana-Purdue University who studies the biology of leatherback turtles at Las Baulas National Park, Guanacaste, Costa Rica. The volunteers depicted in Chapter 1 are from Earthwatch Institute, a nonprofit organization. Earthwatch supports field science and conservation through the participation of the public. See **www.earthwatch.org** for more information.

Table of
CONTENTS

Dr. Frank Paladino studies leatherback turtles, the largest turtles in the world.

BETWEEN LAND AND SEA

Dr. Frank Paladino

is walking along a tropical beach
at night with two assistants.
They have only the moonlight
to guide them along a curved
stretch of sand. The beach is
quiet, except for the warm sea
breeze rustling the palms and the
swish-swish of the surf.

In the dim distance, the group sees a dark shape emerging from the water. As they walk closer, the team sees that the creature is huge. It is nearly six feet long and heavier than all three people put together. The giant reptile slowly hauls itself onto the beach. Dr. Paladino and his team reach the animal as it stops to rest. They click on their headlamps and find themselves face-to-face with a leatherback turtle.

Leatherback turtles are the largest turtles in the world. They are also the deepest diving reptiles, plunging more than 4,000 feet below the surface. They swim thousands of miles in a year. Although they are graceful swimmers, the sea turtles are slow-moving on land. Even so, every two to four years, the females return to tropical beaches around the world for one reason: to nest. There, on the border between land and sea, the turtles dig a deep hole for their eggs. Without sandy beaches, sea turtles would have nowhere to nest.

A Tide of Turtles

"I think I see another one farther up the beach," says Dr. Paladino, pointing across the moonlit sand. He kneels next to the turtle in front of them. "This could be a long night. We'd better get to work."

The giant turtle begins to dig a nest hole in the beach with her powerful flippers. As she does this, she goes into a sort of trance. Dr. Paladino and one

A female leatherback turtle covers her nest early in the morning.

◊ 7 ◊

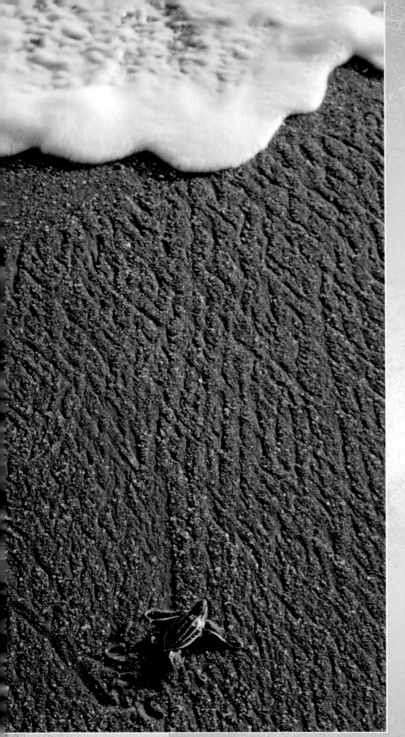

assistant work together to measure the turtle's huge shell and its flippers. The other assistant writes down the turtle's measurements and the location of the nest. Dr. Paladino puts a metal tag on one of the turtle's flippers. When she returns to nest again, they will know her by this tag.

"This one should come back five or six more times this season," says Dr. Paladino. "Then, with a little luck, we'll see her here again in three years."

When the turtle finishes digging a deep, round hole, she starts laying eggs into it.

One person counts them, gently catching each egg and letting it fall into the nest. The eggs are soft, and nearly as big as a billiard ball. The turtle lays sixty-one of them. Then she covers the nest with sand before dragging her heavy body to the water again. In about two months, the hatchlings will find the same path to the sea.

The Edge of the Earth

Sea turtles are just one of the many different kinds of animals that spend time on sandy beaches or rocky shorelines. Animals from both the land and sea can be found along the shore.

Scientists come to the seashore as well. They study the important role of the seashore biome in the lives of plants and animals. For example, Dr. Paladino measures and tags nesting leatherbacks and counts their eggs. With this information, he hopes to understand how well the sea turtle population is doing, and how people can help it grow.

Leatherback turtle hatchlings scurry to the sea as soon as they hatch, after growing inside eggs for two months.

WHAT IS A BIOME?

Seashores are one kind of biome. A biome is a large region of the earth where certain plants and animals live. They survive there because they are well suited to the environment found in that area.

Each biome has plants that may not be found in other biomes. Tall trees grow in forests, but not in deserts. Green algae grow along the coast, but

sand crab

not in the deep sea. The animals that eat these plants help form the living communities of a biome. Learning about biomes is a good way to begin to understand how these communities work. In this book you will learn about the seashore biome and the plants and animals that live there.

The MAKING OF A SEASHORE

Seashores are found

wherever land meets the salty ocean.
The ground can be smooth sand
or rugged rock. Seashores follow
the edge of the sea, from the
frozen shores of the Arctic Ocean
to the tropical beaches of the
Caribbean Sea. If you could
straighten out all the world's

THE SEASHORE

Some seashores have sandy beaches (below) while others have rocky beaches (right).

seashores in a line they would reach as far as 600,000 miles (1,000,000 kilometers). That's almost twenty-five times as far as the distance around the world. Each stretch of seashore is different, molded by the changing land and sea around them.

The Crashing Waves

The sound of crashing or lapping waves and the smell of salt spray are familiar signs of the seashore. The water also helps shape the seashores. Along rocky

shores, storms and giant waves crash on cliffs, breaking the rocks apart bit by bit. At sandy beaches, mighty currents sweep along the shore. The currents move sand from one place to another. Howling winds build sand dunes and coat everything with salt spray.

The shape of the seashore is always changing. Because it is pounded by wave after wave, the seashore can be a tough place for plants and animals to live. Plants have a hard time finding solid ground

in which to put their roots. Animals must deal with the constant action of the waves. At first glance, you might think that there is no life among the rocks and sand. But with a close look, you will see all kinds of living things in this biome.

Gifts From the Sea

The same waves that break rocks apart and move beaches also bring life-giving nutrients to the seashore. Nutrients are chemicals that plants and animals need to live and grow. The ocean is full of nutrients, in the form of living plants and animals, as well as those that have died. Each wave brings a new flood of nutrients from the ocean onto the land.

The first sign of these gifts from the sea is the line of broken seaweed, sea grass, and other floating matter on the beach. This line marks the high-tide line, which is a great source of nutrients for beach animals. Dead fish, shellfish, and other creatures are tangled among the seaweed. They are a feast for

sand dunes

high tide line

some beach animals such as crabs. The waves also bring tiny bits of decaying seaweed and animals. These bits filter down through the sand and feed a whole community of tiny animals living there.

Animals bring nutrients from the ocean onto shore, too. Birds that hunt at sea come to shore to tear apart their food. They also may leave feces on land, which certain tiny animals depend on for survival. Even sea turtles, which spend most of their

The high tide line contains seaweed and other bits of ocean life that beach animals can eat.

lives feeding at sea, come on to beaches to lay their eggs. When the eggs hatch, many of the hatchlings become food for gulls and other shorebirds. When a massive whale strands itself on the beach, it will feed other animals for weeks.

The Rising Tide

Tides are the rising and falling of the sea level. All seashores are affected by the tides. There is a low tide and a high tide. The high-tide line is the highest point that the tide reaches. The low-tide line is the lowest level of the tide. Perhaps the most important part of seashores for plants and animals is the area between the high-tide line and the low-tide line. This area is called the intertidal zone.

Tide pools are special areas in the intertidal zone. They are hollows, like miniature ponds, in the rock or sand. They stay full of water, even at low tide. Plants and animals that need water can survive there when the land around them is dry at low tide.

Tide pools are exciting because you can see animals that would normally be hard to find, such as sea stars, sea urchins, hermit crabs, and fish. They find some safety in the tiny pools, which are too small for large predators.

Living things in the seashore biome aren't always so noticeable. They are often burrowed in the sand

Tide pools are pockets of water that stay full, even during low tide. The pools can protect smaller animals from larger animals that might eat them.

◇ 17 ◇

or clinging to a wet rock. Still, seashores are a fascinating place to learn about how living communities work.

SEASHORE FACTS

✓ **Found around the world:** Wherever land meets sea, from the tropics to the poles, there will be a seashore.

✓ **Carved by waves:** Wave action shapes seashores, which are always changing.

✓ **Piles of sand:** Sand from the ocean is deposited on the shore to make sandy beaches. Wind shapes the sand into dunes.

✓ **All washed up:** Seashores receive nutrients from the sea, in the form of plants, animals, and particles from the ocean floor.

✓ **Between high and low:** The intertidal zone, between high and low tide, is rich in life.

SEASHORE COMMUNITIES

Like biomes on land,

seashores are made of communities of plants and animals. Communities are the groups of living things found together in a place. Each living thing has a role in the community. Many of the plants and animals depend on others.

THE SEASHORE

Energy Flow at the Seashore

Seashore plants, such as brown algae and beach grass, trap the sun's energy for their food. They use the energy to make sugars from water and carbon dioxide (a gas in the air and dissolved in the water). They store the sugars and use the energy later when they need it to grow.

Beach grass uses the sun's energy to make food.

Some animals have to eat plants to get their energy. Animals that eat only plants are called herbivores. Sea urchins and snails are examples of herbivores in the seashore biome. Animals that eat other animals are called carnivores. Sea stars, gulls, and sculpins are carnivores. Carnivores get their energy from eating the meat of other animals. Some animals, such as hermit crabs, eat both plants and animals. They are called omnivores.

In the intertidal zone, another source of food is all around at high tide. These are tiny plants and animals called plankton. Plankton float through the water for any animal to eat. Like larger animals,

The purple sea urchin is one herbivore that lives at the seashore. Here it is eating kelp, a kind of brown algae.

A gull dines on a starfish. Gulls are carnivores.

plankton animals (zooplankton) eat plankton plants (phytoplankton) to get their energy. A large number of animals in the intertidal zone sift plankton from the water for their food. They include barnacles, sponges, and clams.

Other animals get their energy from dead plants and animals. They break down the plants and animals and use their nutrients. Crabs and other detritus eaters do this job. They are called detritivores.

The Food Web

The flow of energy through the seashore from the sun to plants to herbivores to carnivores and detritivores follows a pattern called a food web. Like a spider's web, it is a complicated network of who eats whom. The web connects all the plants and animals of a particular community. For instance, at the seashore, snails eat algae. Gulls, in turn, eat snails. When a gull dies, blue crabs may eat its meat.

These tiny plankton animals, or zooplankton, live in the ocean. Many animals eat these zooplankton.

Together, plants and animals pass energy through the biome community. They also use some of the energy to live. At each stage of the food web, some energy is lost as the animals use it. It is lost in the form of heat. More energy from the sun has to be trapped by plants to keep the community alive.

By looking at the plants and animals of the seashore biome, you will see how they may rely on one another. If you take any plant or animal away, it could change how the community works.

SUNLIGHT

USED BY

PLANTS ~~~ HEAT LOSS

EATEN BY

HERBIVORES ~~~ HEAT LOSS

EATEN BY

CARNIVORES ~~~ HEAT LOSS

DETRITIVORES
eat dead plants
and animals

Chapter 4

SEASHORE PLANTS

The plants of the seashore are not always easy to see. The rocks and sand will not support arching forests, so the beach may look empty of anything green. Yet there are actually many plants at the seashore, large and small. They are all part of the seashore community.

Shifting Ground

At the edge of the water, the sand is constantly shifting with the waves and the tide. There is no solid ground in which roots can take hold. Instead, millions of tiny plants live among the grains of sand. They include blue-green algae and diatoms. Diatoms are single-celled algae with hard shells. These plants are so small, you need a microscope to see each

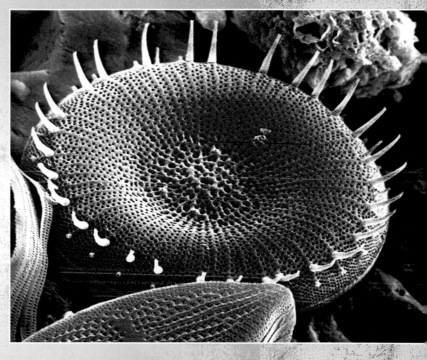

one. They live in the upper layers of sand, where they can soak in energy from the sunlight. When the high tide rolls in, they are covered in the nutrient-rich waters they need to survive.

Larger plants can find refuge in the more stable sands found below the low-tide line. There, eelgrass,

Diatoms, like this one shown under a microscope, are made of just one cell. They are small, but they are an important food for many seashore animals.

Eelgrass grows in the shallow water at the seashore. It can capture the sun's energy to make food.

sea grass, or larger algae (seaweed) may form large mats of green. They live where the waters are shallow enough for the sun to reach them.

Firm Footing

Rocky shores are a great place for algae to grow. These simple plants don't need soil or roots to get their water and nutrients. Everything they need is in the water around them. They have a special part,

called a holdfast, that attaches them firmly to the rock.

Red algae cover the lowest regions of rocky shores at the water's edge. These areas are seen only at low tide. Above them on the rocks, brown algae called rockweeds grow. They are mixed in with other algae. Higher on the rocks, where only the highest tides reach, a band of blue-green algae often grows. Fewer plants grow on rocky shores above the high-tide line, an area battered by ocean waves. There, a band of bright orange and gray lichens may cling tightly to the rocks.

At low tide, most algae of the intertidal zone look limp, but in tide pools, all kinds of algae wave in the water. These algae give shelter and food to the many animals also found in tide pools.

Low tide on the rocky beach: algae (top), black mussels, and sandy-colored barnacles.

◆ 29 ◆

On tropical seashores, palm trees grow along the beach.

Trees by the Seas

Farther back from the crashing waves and tides of the ocean, more plants are able to grow on the seashore. Palm trees sway at the edge of tropical beaches in Florida and California. Spruce and fir trees line northern seashores, as in Maine, Oregon, and

Canada. Oaks and pines grow along warmer coasts, such as in South Carolina.

On sandy beaches, the wind blows the sand into rolling hills called dunes. Only the toughest plants can grow there. The wind is strong and the salt spray from the ocean dries out leaves. Grasses

SEASHORE PLANTS

Spruce trees grow along cool, rocky seashores.

Plants grow in the dunes away from the water's edge on this beach in Texas. Their strong roots help them stand up to the strong wind.

such as beach grass and beach pea grow on dunes closest to the beach. They have deep, spreading roots. Farther from the beach, the dunes are more sheltered. Plants like beach heather and seaside goldenrod grow among the grasses. Shrubs such as bayberry and rose grow in the most protected spots. Even farther from the beach, oaks and other trees may grow on the dunes. They are not the tall,

straight trees found in forests. They tend to be short and bent by the wind and the constant salt spray.

From dunes to the rocky intertidal zone, the plants of the seashore form the basis for the coastal food chain. They provide food for the many animals of the seashore, both in the water and out.

SEASHORE PLANTS

✓**Tiny plants:**
Although sandy beaches can't support many large plants, they have many tiny blue-green algae and diatoms living in them.

✓**Stripes of life:**
Plants grow in distinct bands in the rocky intertidal zone, based on the conditions.

✓**Hanging on:**
Hardy grasses with spreading roots grow on dunes closest to the beach.

✓**Finding shelter:**
Dunes behind the first row of dunes can support larger plants, including herbs, shrubs, and trees.

Chapter 5

SEASHORE ANIMALS

Many of the animals of the seashore are tiny. There may be thousands of them in a handful of sand. Seashores are also an important habitat for many larger animals, at least for part of their lives. For instance, three quarters of all waterbirds that migrate, such as sandpipers and plovers, depend on beaches during their migration trips.

On the Beach

Some of the animals on sandy beaches are as small as grains of sand. For example, sand fleas live in the line of broken seaweed at the high-tide line. Sand fleas are tiny shrimplike animals with many legs. They come out at dusk to feed on rotting bits of plants and animals among the seaweed. Tiny round worms, called nematodes, feed on blue-green algae, diatoms, and bits of detritus (dead plant and animal matter) tucked between the sand grains.

Sanderlings gather along the tide line in search of food.

Horseshoe crabs eat
animals in the sand.

Tardigrades, also known as water bears, poke holes in diatoms and suck out their insides.

Larger animals also burrow in the shifting sand under the pounding waves. Mole crabs follow the tide as it moves up and down the beach. They feed on detritus in the swirling surf. Then they dive back into the sand for the next wave. Ghost crabs burrow in the sand during the day. At night, these crabs scuttle across the sand in search of dead plants and animals to eat. Surf clams are large clams that live just under the surface of the sand. They suck water into their body to sift out bits of dead plant and animal matter.

Many predators come in with high tide to feast on the sand animals. Sand shrimp, green crabs, horseshoe crabs, and even larger fish such as flounder and skates find their dinner in the intertidal zone. Moon snails glide along the sand at high tide in search of small clams. Other predators live in the

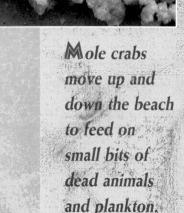

Mole crabs move up and down the beach to feed on small bits of dead animals and plankton.

sand all the time. Clam worms and sandworms, worms with bristly legs, are voracious predators.

Shorebirds also eat animals living in the sandy intertidal zone. Sanderlings, sandpipers, plovers, curlews, dowitchers, and other birds have long legs and long beaks to feed at the water's edge. There they find worms, clams, sand shrimp, and a feast of other animals. Gulls break open large mollusks such as surf clams by dropping them on nearby rocks. They also eat most of the dead fish or other animals that wash up on shore.

A clam worm is a predator that lives in the sand at the seashore.

On the Rocks

Animals are easier to find on rocky shores than on sandy beaches, because there they are not able to burrow in the sand. Barnacles are usually found clustered in groups on rocks in the intertidal zone. They are thick-shelled animals that cement themselves tightly to the rock. Barnacles have two plates that open at high tide. This allows them to wave their feathery arms in the water to catch and feed on plankton. At low tide, the plates are clamped shut, making the barnacles look more like part of the rock.

Blue-black mussels grow in clusters among the rockweed. They are held down by tough threads. Like barnacles, they wait until high tide to open up and feed. They suck water through their bodies to filter out plankton.

All the algae in the rocky intertidal zone do not go unnoticed by herbivores. Snails called periwinkles and limpets graze on algae, like cows graze on grass.

Many animals in the intertidal zone can be found in colorful tide pools.

Sea urchins munch on all kinds of algae in protected tide pools. Other small animals live among the rockweed but feed on detritus and plankton in the water. These include tiny shrimplike animals, coiled tubeworms, and hydroids. The hydroids have a ring of stinging arms that they use to trap plankton.

Larger predators feed on barnacles and mussels. Dog whelks are predatory snails with bumpy shells. They drill holes in mussels to get to their flesh.

They inject barnacles with a poison and pry their two plates apart to eat them. Green crabs and sea stars also feed on mussels when the tide is high.

You can find all the animals of the intertidal zone in rocky tide pools. Barnacles grow alongside flowerlike sea anemones and bright green and yellow sponges. Sea urchins and periwinkles graze on the algae in the tide pool. Sea squirts suck water through themselves to filter out plankton. Roving predators, like hermit crabs, green crabs, and sea stars, stalk prey in the little pools.

mussel

barnacles

A dog whelk can drill a hole into a mussel to eat its flesh.

Northern elephant seals rest on the seashore.

Seashore Visitors

Seashores are important to other animals that are not always found there. For many of these, the seashore is a safe place to rest or nest. Seals haul up on beaches and rocky shores to rest. Some fish, such as sand lance and surf smelt, swim to the beach

during high tides and lay their eggs in the sand. Plovers and terns nest in the dunes of sandy beaches. Other seabirds nest on rocky islands in enormous numbers. Sea turtles, like the leatherbacks studied by Dr. Frank Paladino, struggle onto tropical beaches around the world every year to lay their eggs. All of these animals have an impact on other parts of the ocean as well. However, their life cycles would not be complete without the seashore.

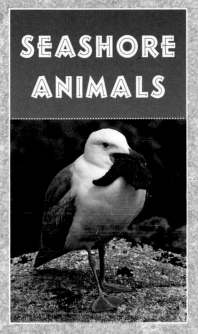

SEASHORE ANIMALS

✓ **Migratory route:** Three quarters of all waterbirds that migrate make use of seashore habitats during their migration.

✓ **Sand life:** Millions of tiny animals, no larger than grains of sand, feast on the detritus and algae found among the sand.

✓ **Waves of plenty:** Predators of sandy beaches, especially shorebirds, find a feast of tiny animals among the shifting tides.

✓ **Floating food:** Many animals on rocky shores take advantage of the feast of plankton and detritus in the water during high tide.

✓ **The water's fine:** Tide pools provide habitat for many animals usually found lower than the intertidal zone, such as sea stars, sea anemones, and sea urchins.

SOME PLANTS AND ANIMALS IN THE
SEASHORE FOOD WEB

PLANTS	HERBIVORES	CARNIVORES
	Eaten by →	**Eaten by** →

PLANTS

Beach grass

Phytoplankton

Diatoms

Rockweed

Green algae

Red algae

HERBIVORES

Seaside grasshoppers

Zooplankton

Nematodes

Tardigrades

Periwinkles

Limpets

Sea urchins

CARNIVORES

Wolf spiders

Barnacles

Sea anemones

Sponges

Clams

Mussels

Dog whelks

Sandworms

Sea stars

Gulls

Sandpipers

Plovers

DETRITIVORES

Sand fleas

Tubeworms

Mole crabs

Crabs

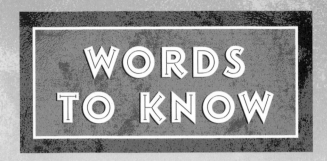

WORDS TO KNOW

barnacle—One of the thick-shelled crustaceans that are permanently attached to rocks in the intertidal zone.

biome—An area defined by the kinds of plants and animals that live there.

carnivore—An animal that eats other animals.

community—All the plants and animals living and interacting in any area.

detritivore—An animal that eats plants and animals after they have died.

detritus—Rotting bits of dead plants and animals.

diatoms—One-celled algae with hard shells of silica.

dunes—Rolling hills of sand deposited by the wind.

food web—The path of energy as it is transferred from the sun and soil to plants to herbivores to carnivores and detritivores, which contribute to the soil again.

habitat—The area in which a certain plant or animal normally lives, eats, and finds shelter.

herbivore—An animal that eats only plants.

intertidal—The region between the water levels at high tide and low tide.

mollusk—An animal related to clams, scallops, snails, octopuses, and squids.

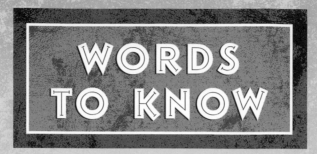

WORDS TO KNOW

nematode—A type of tiny, round worm that lives in the sand.

nutrients—Chemicals necessary for plants and animals to live.

omnivore—An animal that eats both plants and animals.

plankton—Tiny plants and animals, phytoplankton and zooplankton, that float in the water.

rockweed—Brown algae commonly found in the rocky intertidal zone.

tide pool—A depression in the rocky or sandy intertidal zone where water remains, even at low tide.

tides—The rising and falling of the ocean water level in response to the pull of the moon and sun.

LEARN MORE

BOOKS

Nadeau, Isaac. *Food Chains in a Tide Pool Habitat.* New York: PowerKids Press, 2002.

Parker, Steve. DK Eyewitness Books. *Seashore.* New York: DK Publishing, 2004.

Taylor, Barbara. *Seashore Life.* Hauppauge, NY: Barron's Educational Series, 2000.

Wallace, Marianne D. *America's Seashores: Guide to Plants and Animals.* Golden, CO: Fulcrum Publishers, 2005.

INTERNET ADDRESSES

Marine Discovery Centre, Queenscliff. *Intertidal Rocky Shores.* http://www.rockyshores.auz.info/back_info04.htm#

Monterey Bay National Marine Sanctuary. *Virtual Tide Pool* http://www.montereybay.noaa.gov/visitor/TidePool/welcome.html

Office of Naval Research. *Ocean in Motion.* http://www.onr.navy.mil/focus/ocean/motion/default.htm

INDEX